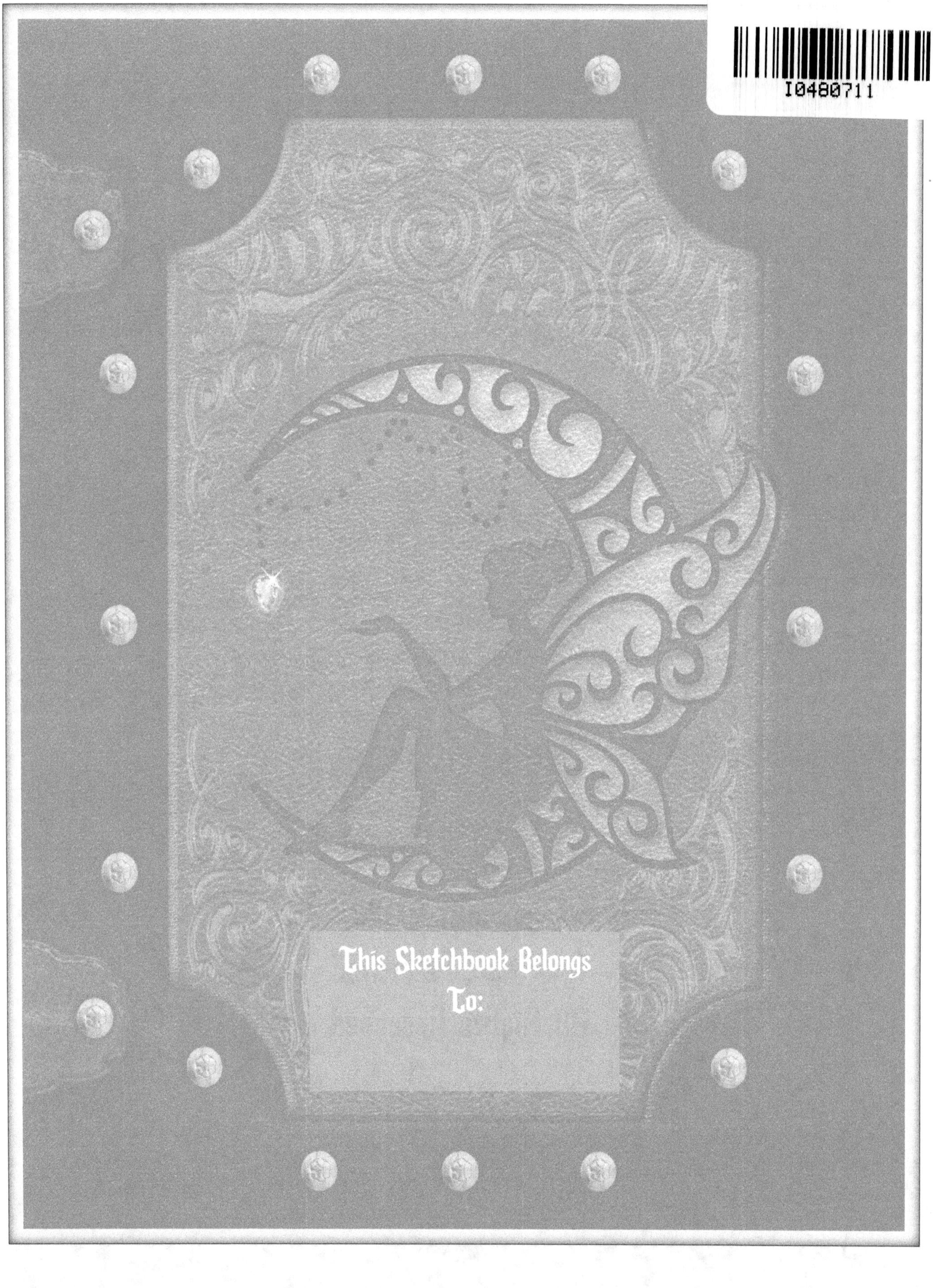
This Sketchbook Belongs
To:

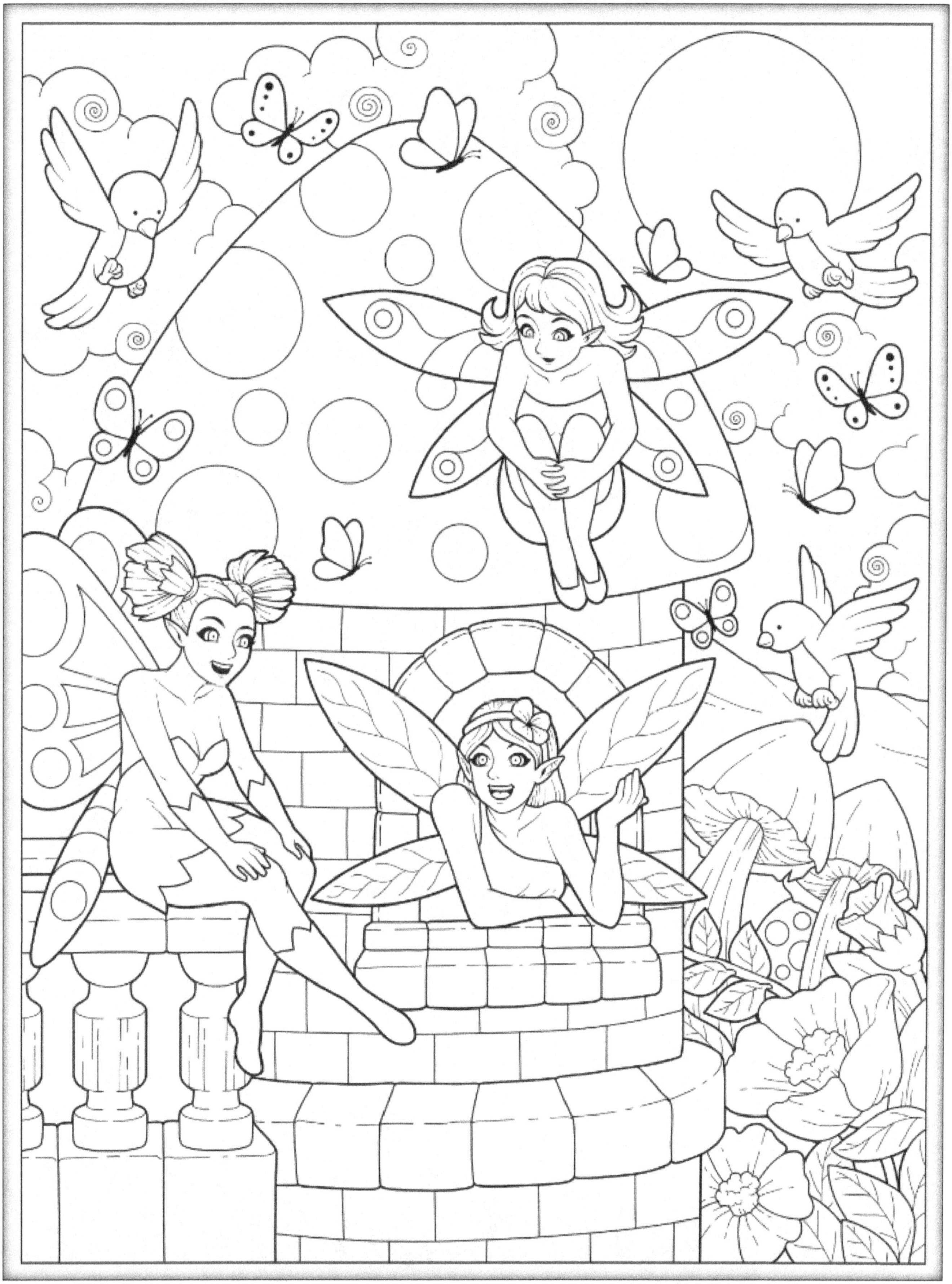

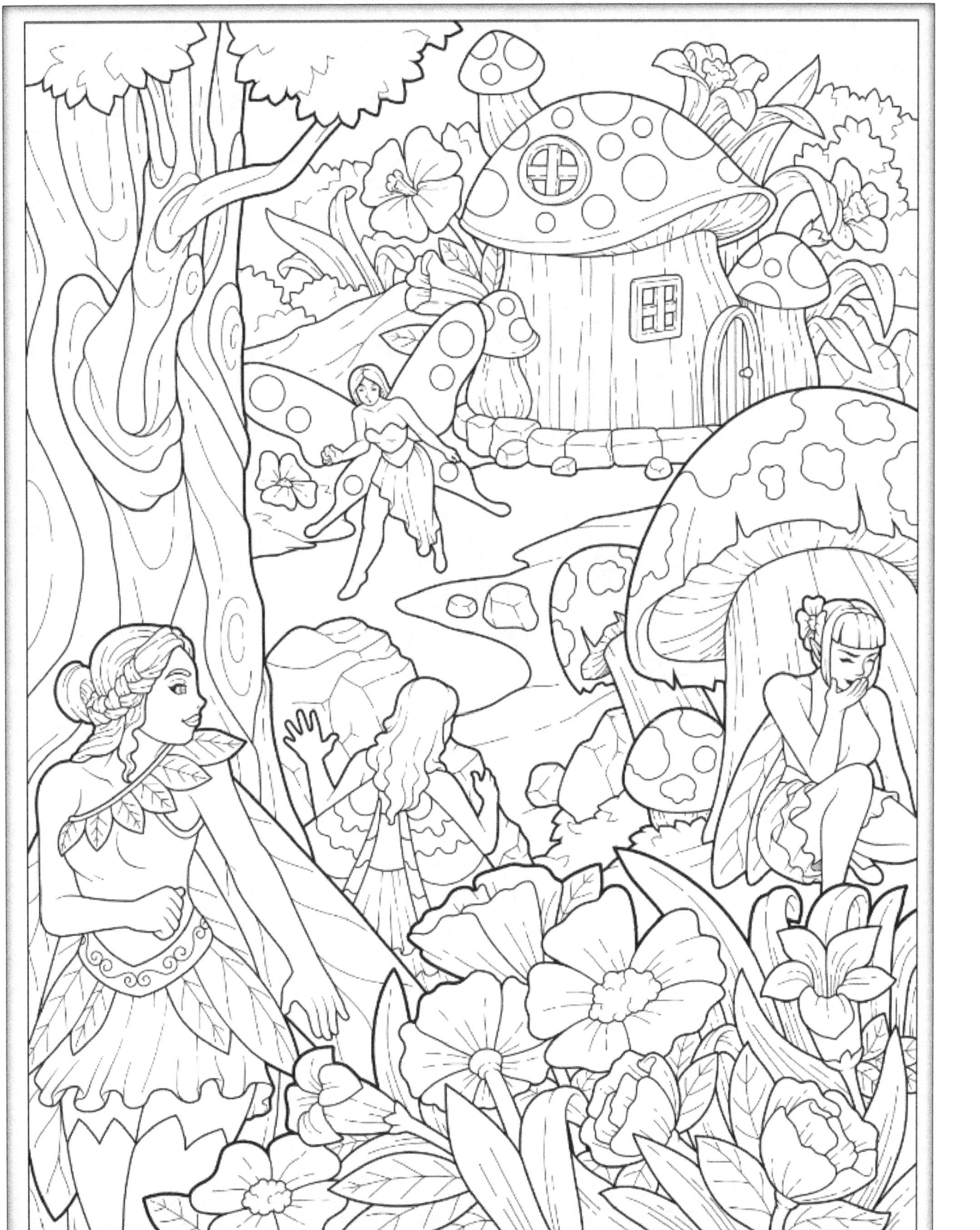

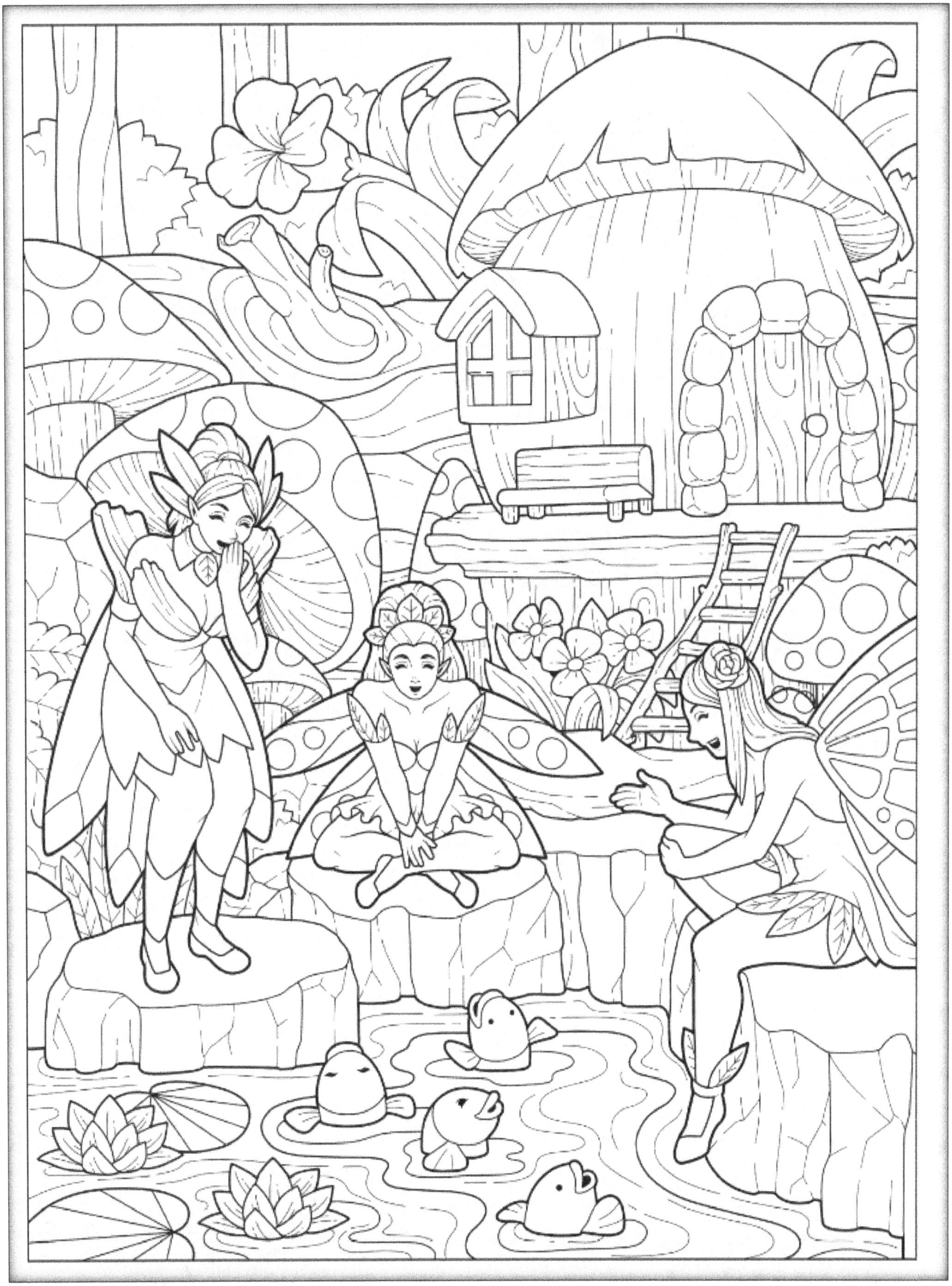

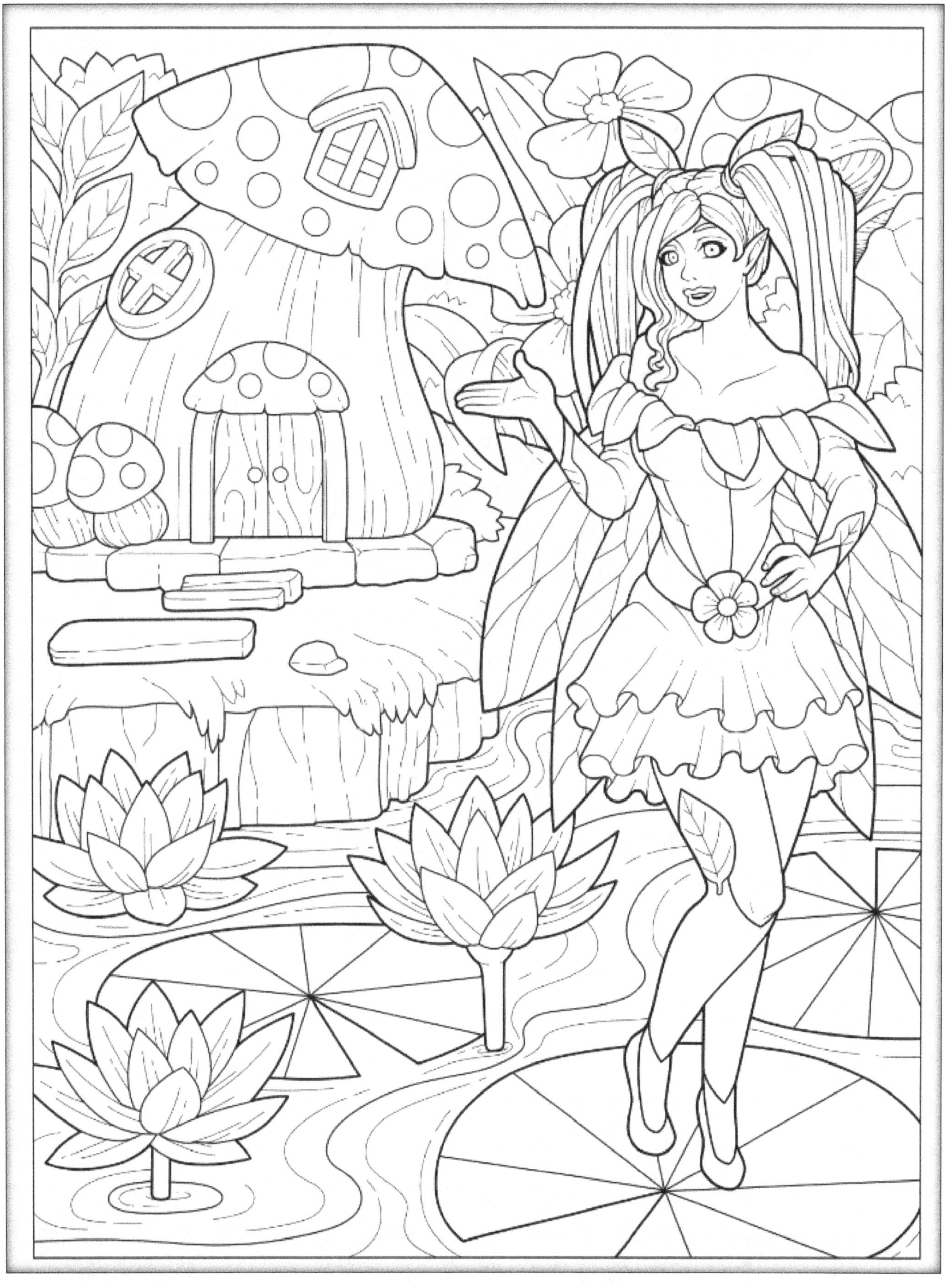

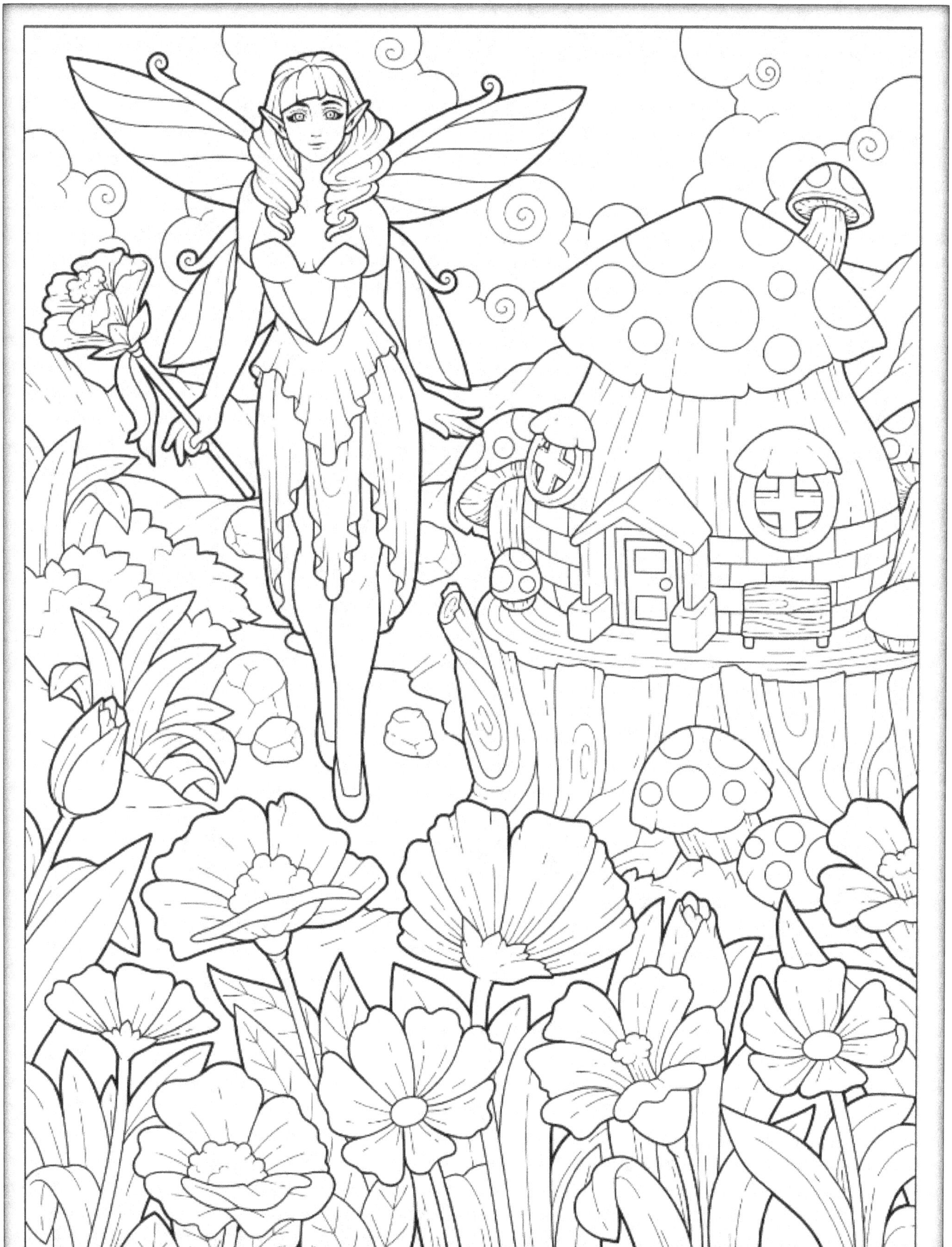

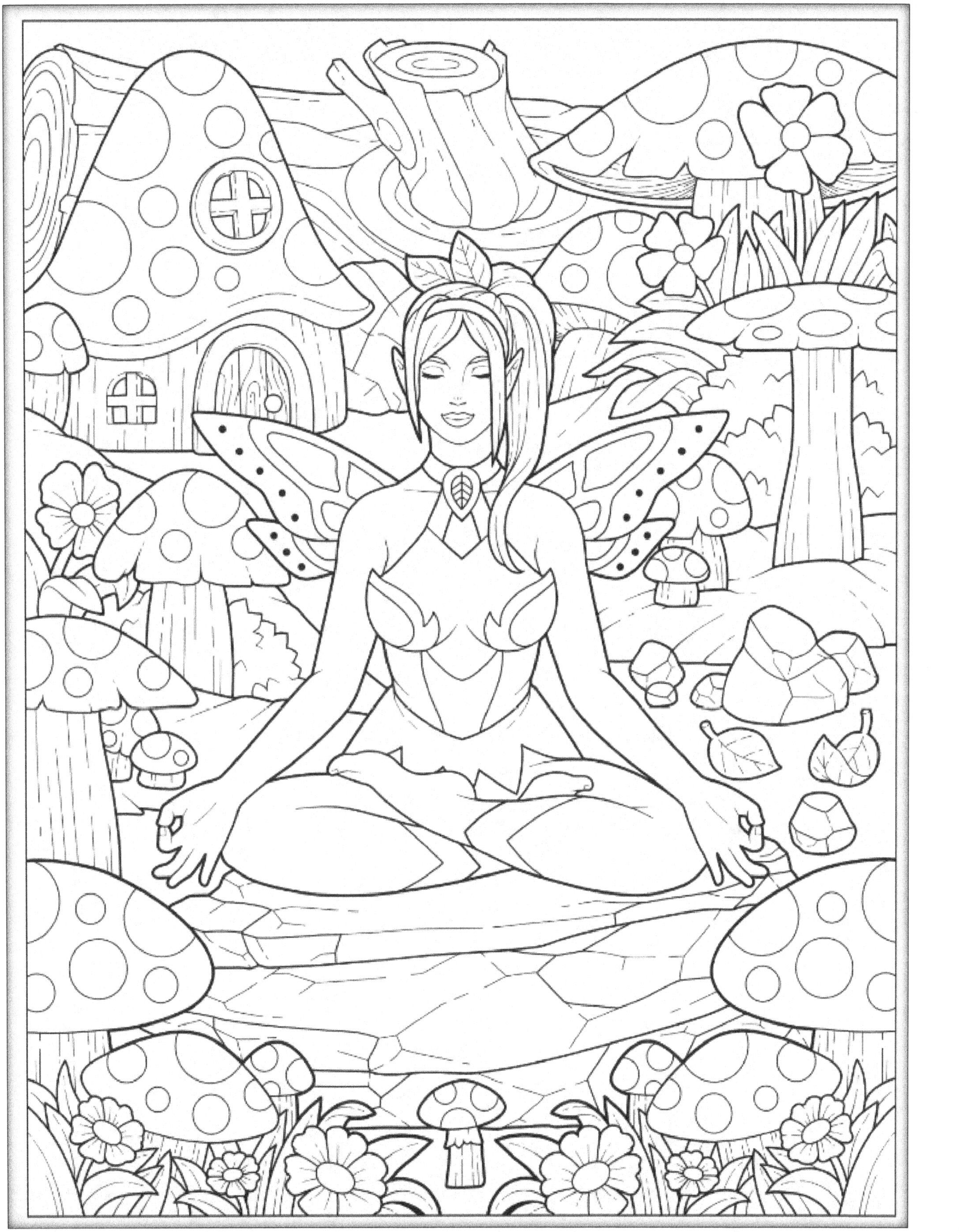

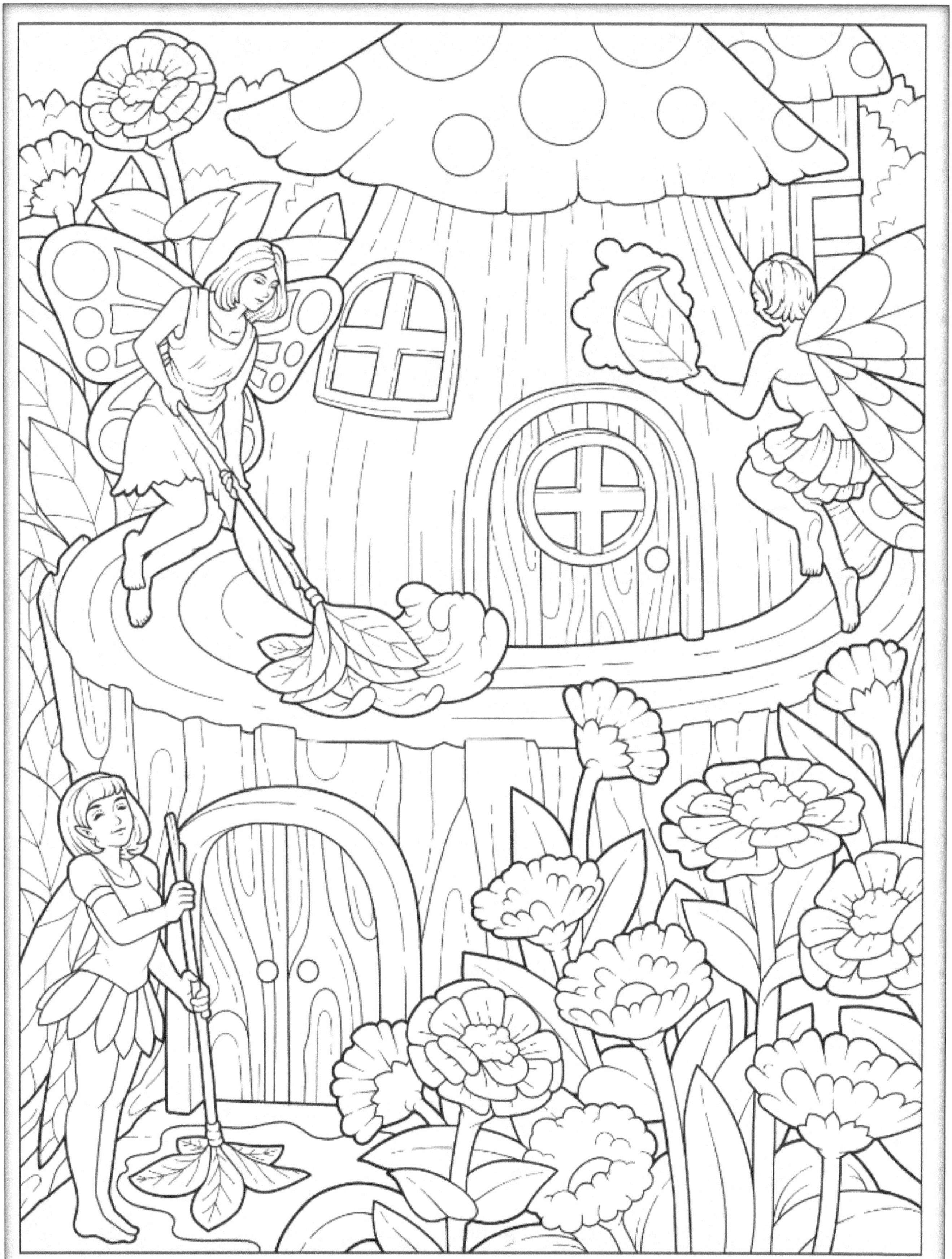

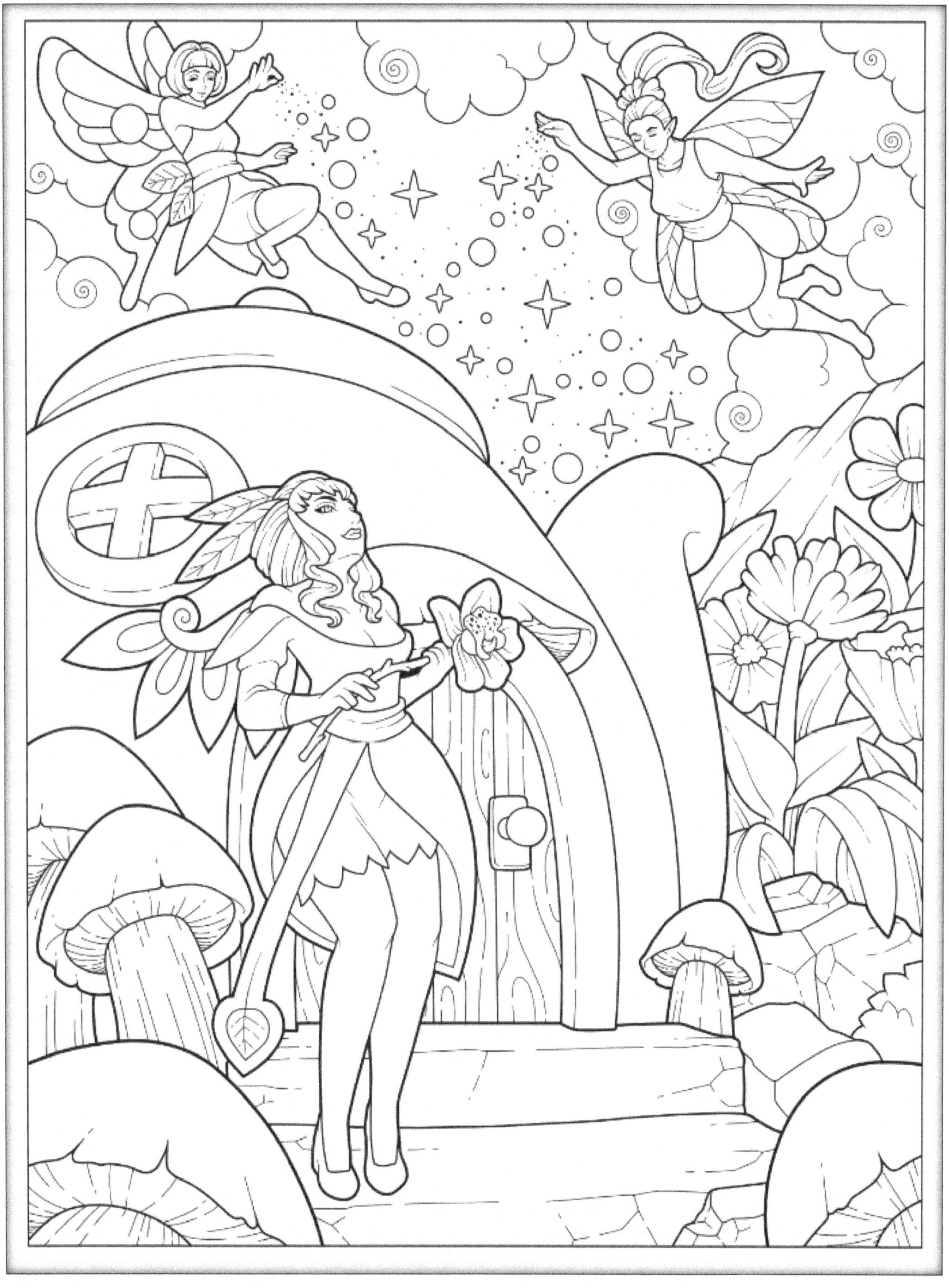

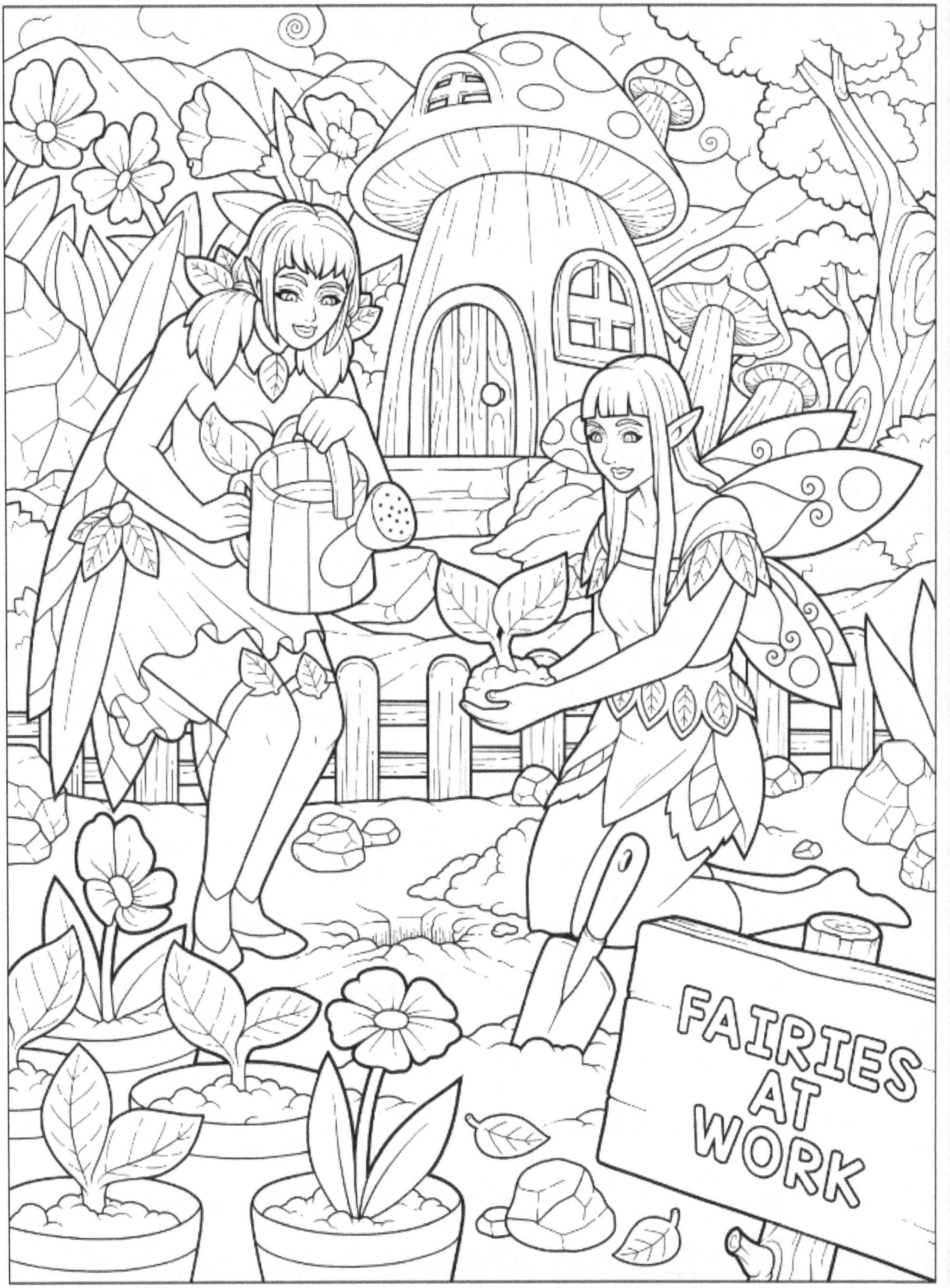
FAIRIES
AT
WORK

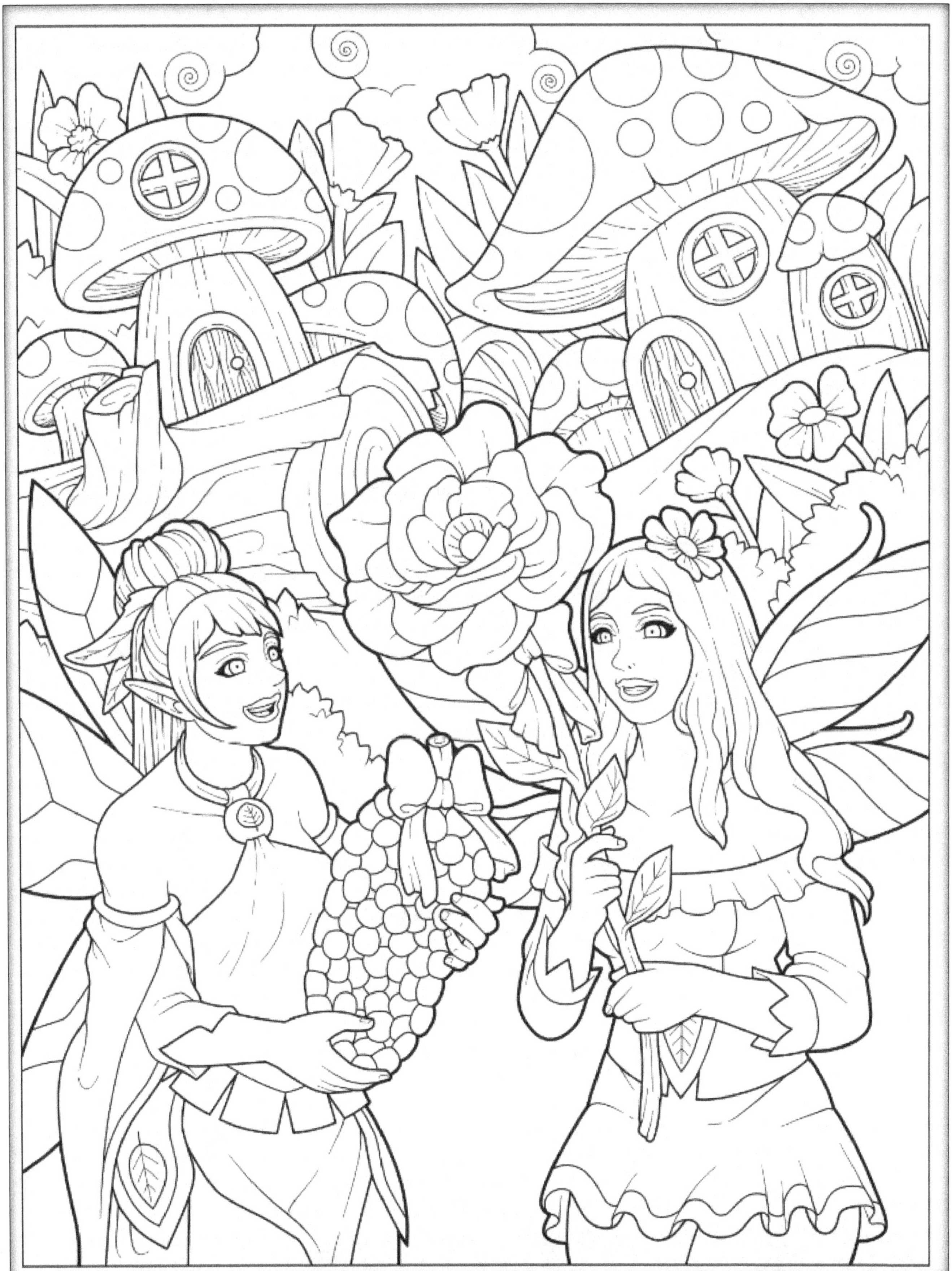

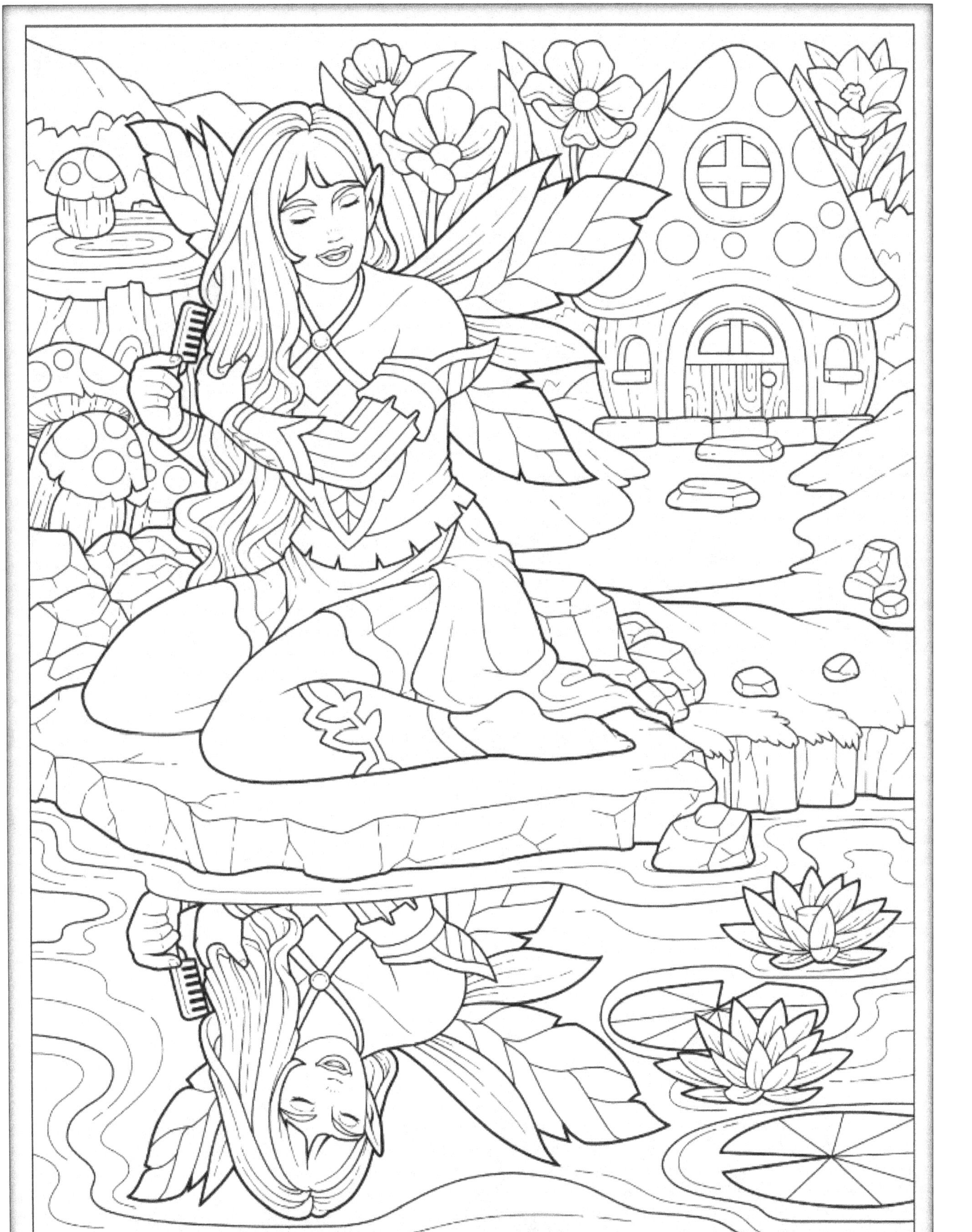

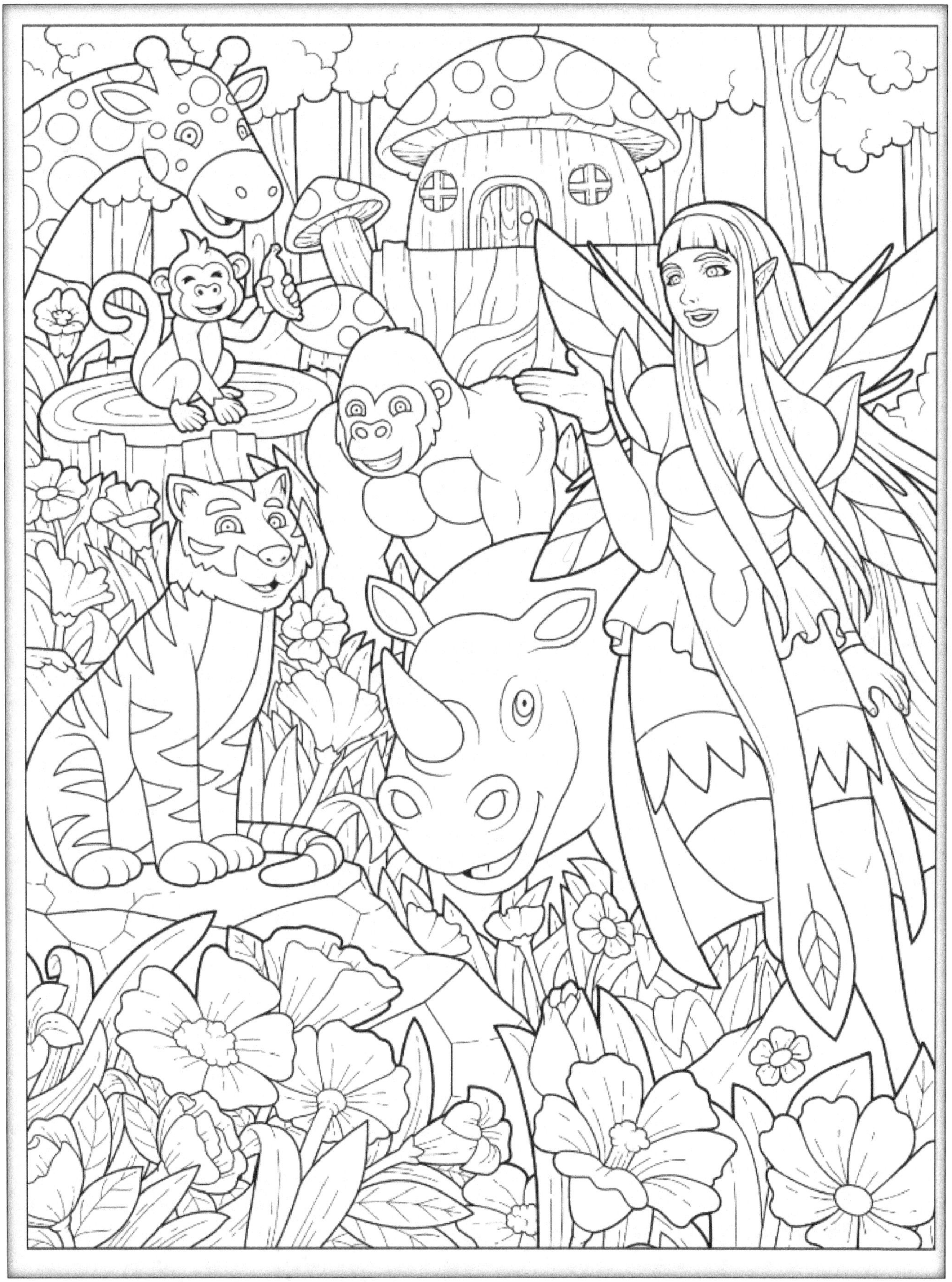

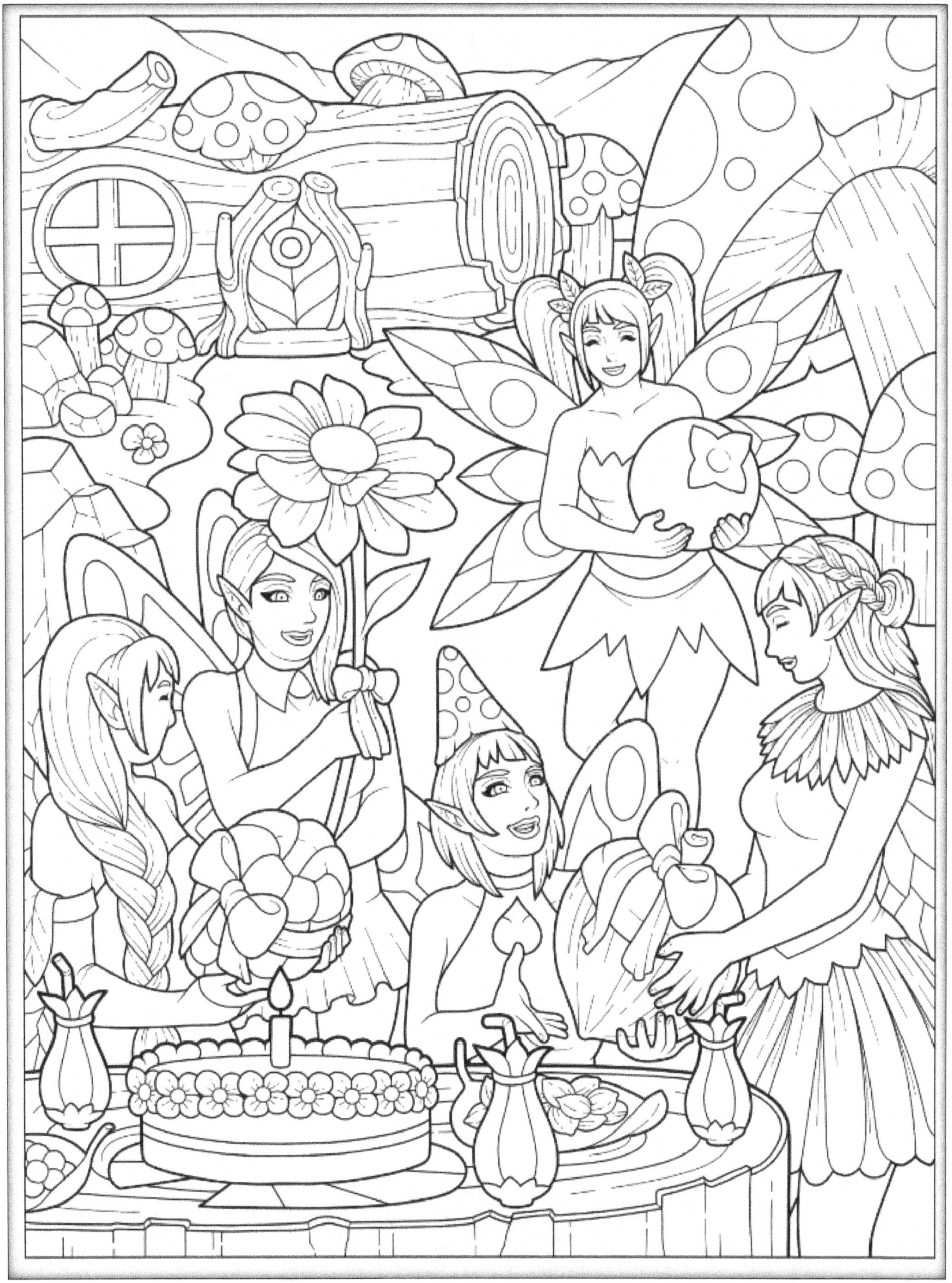

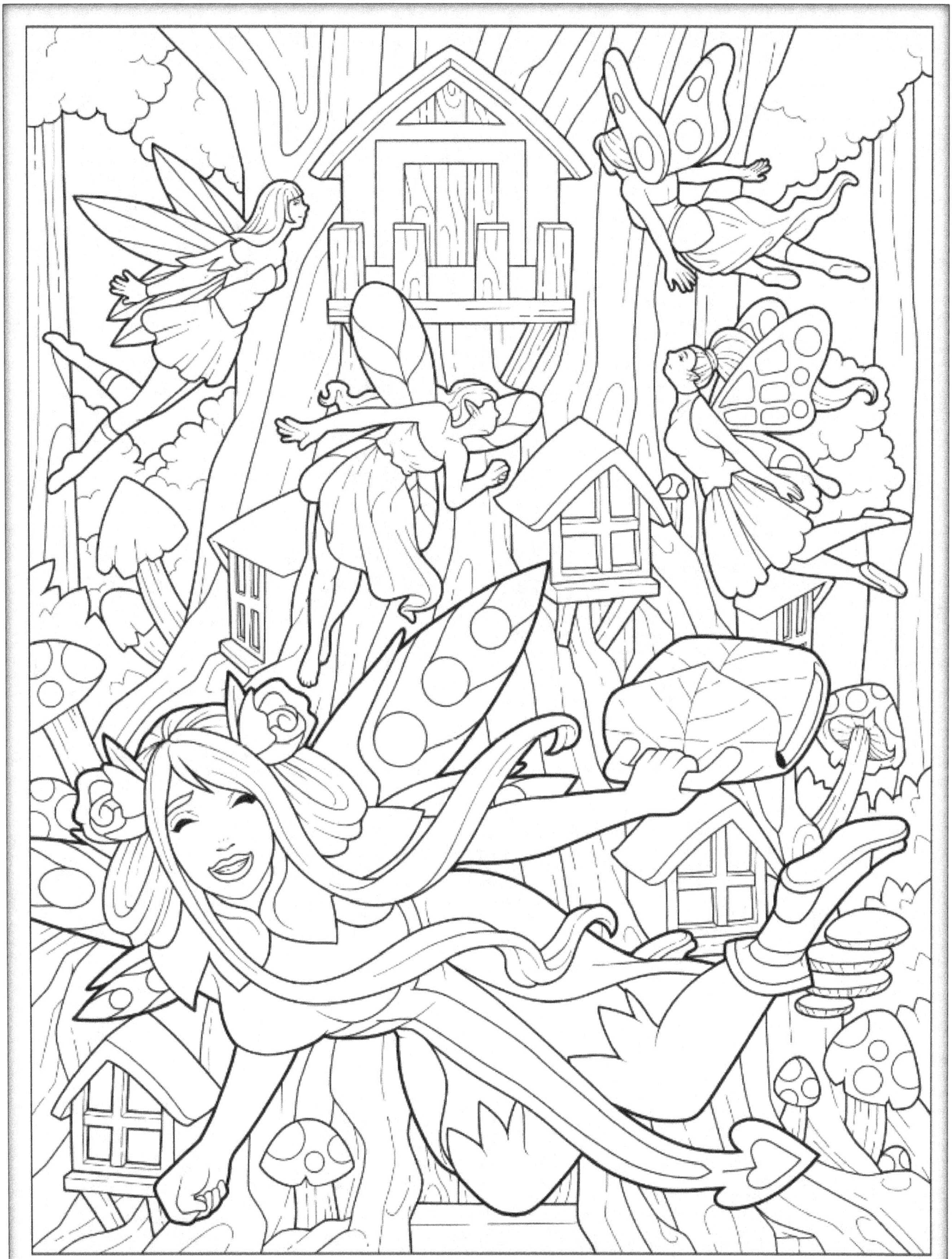

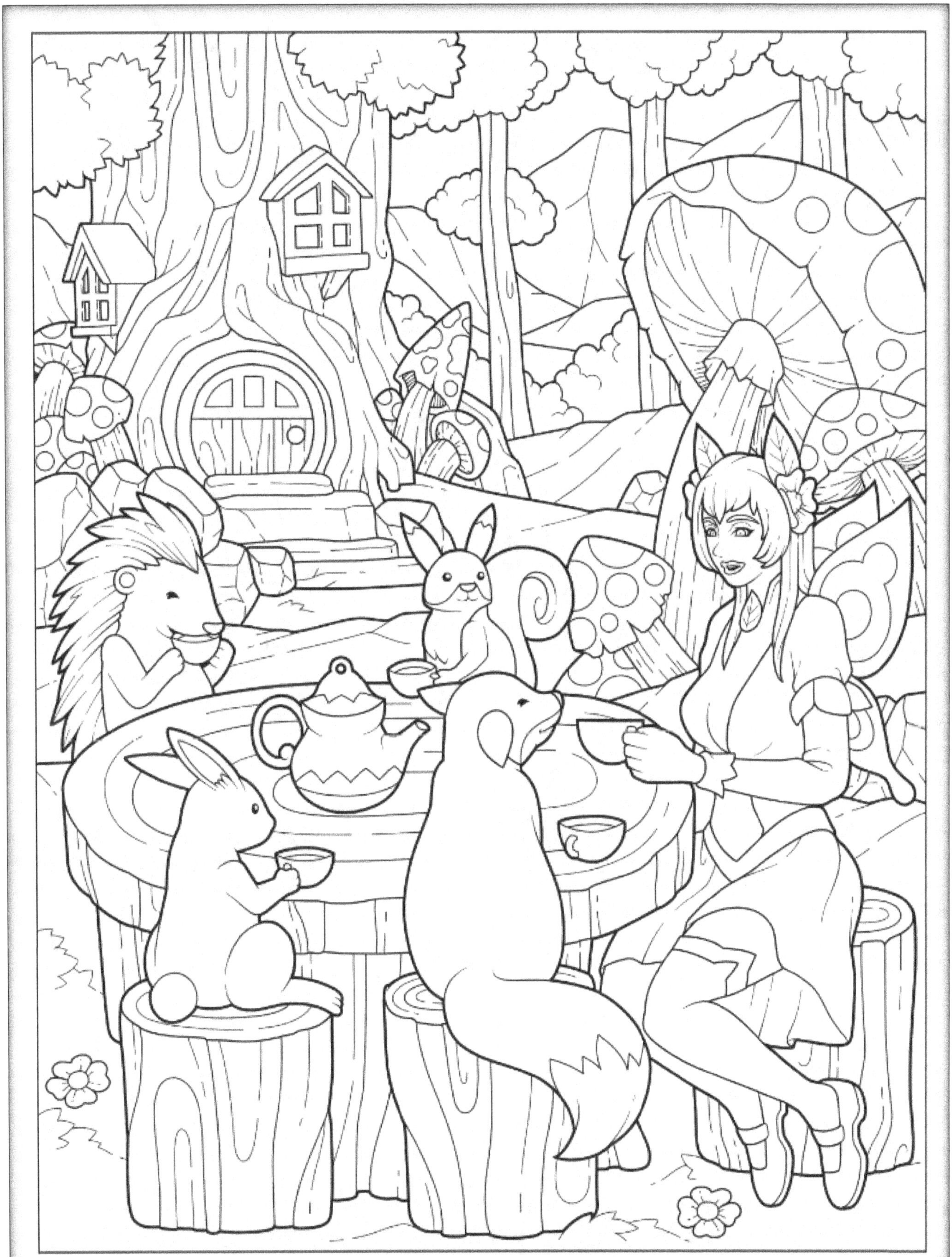

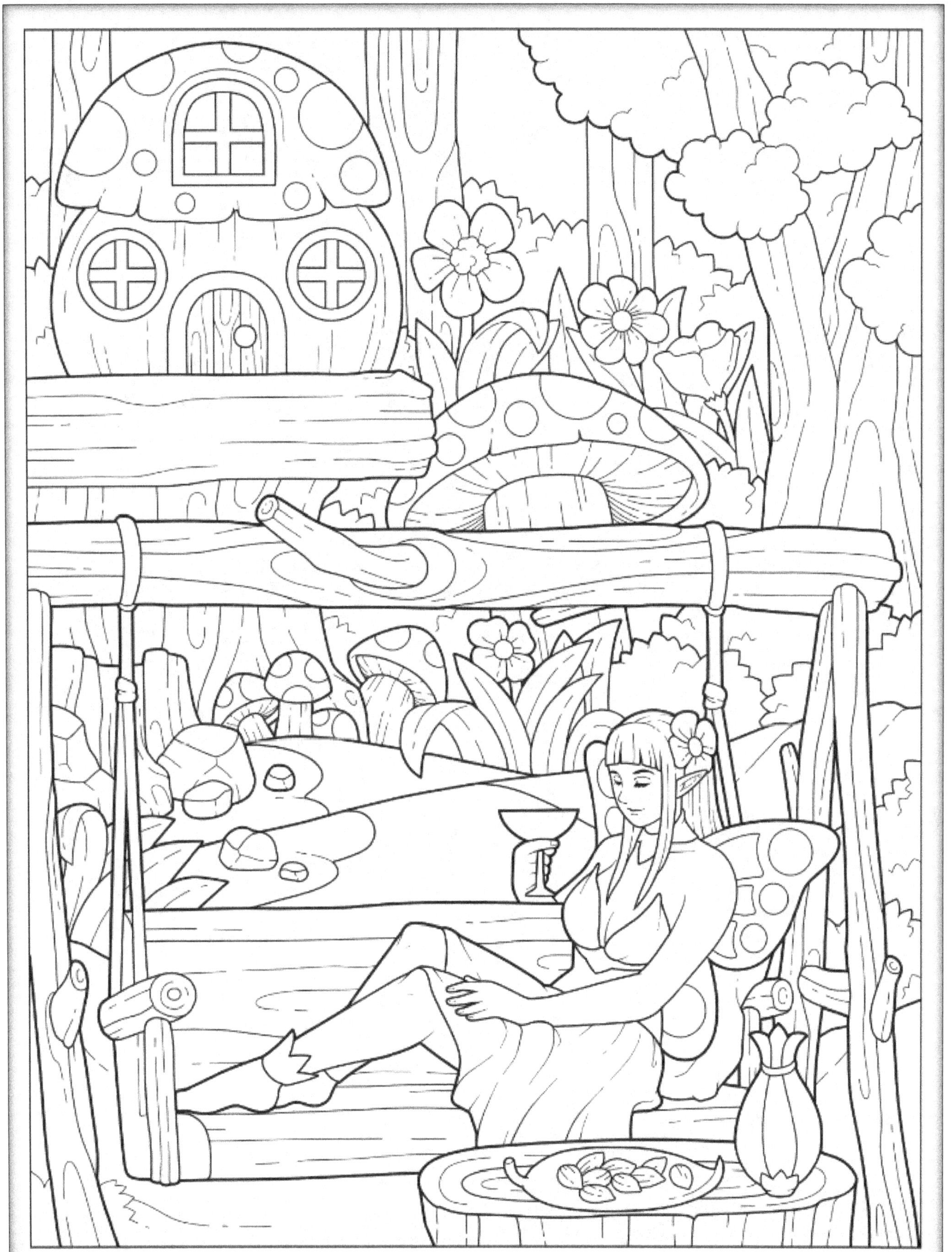

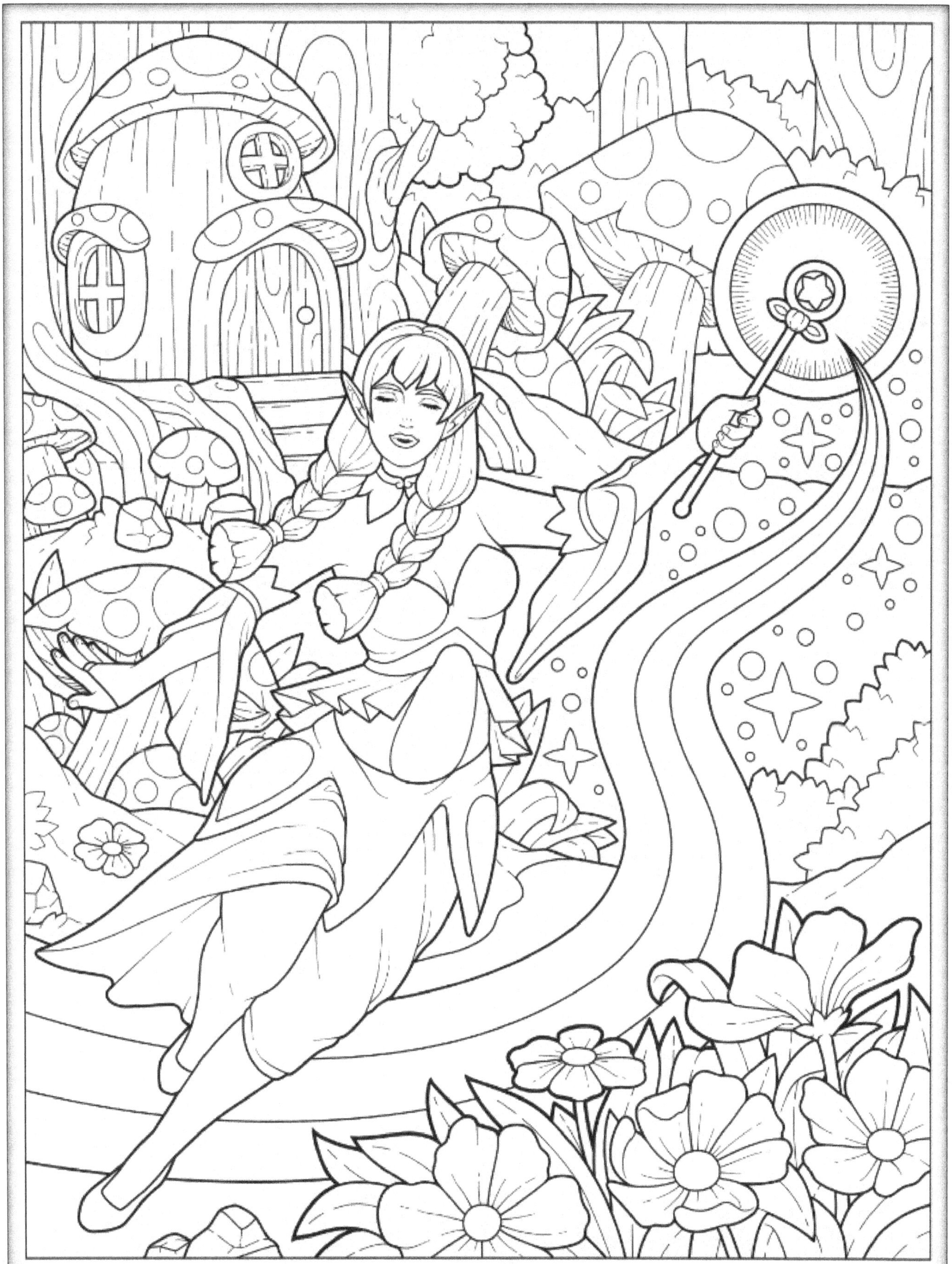

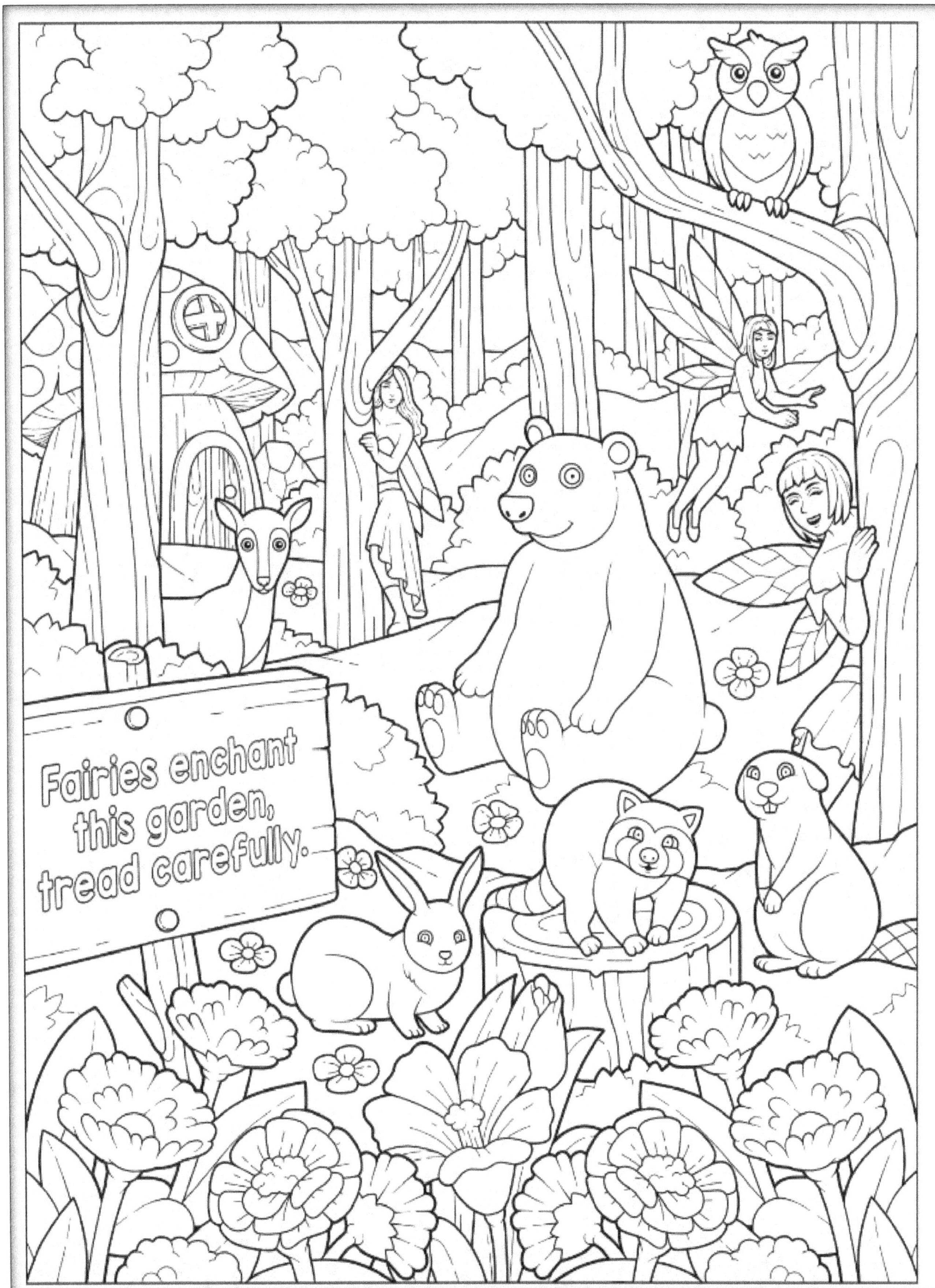
Fairies enchant
this garden,
tread carefully.

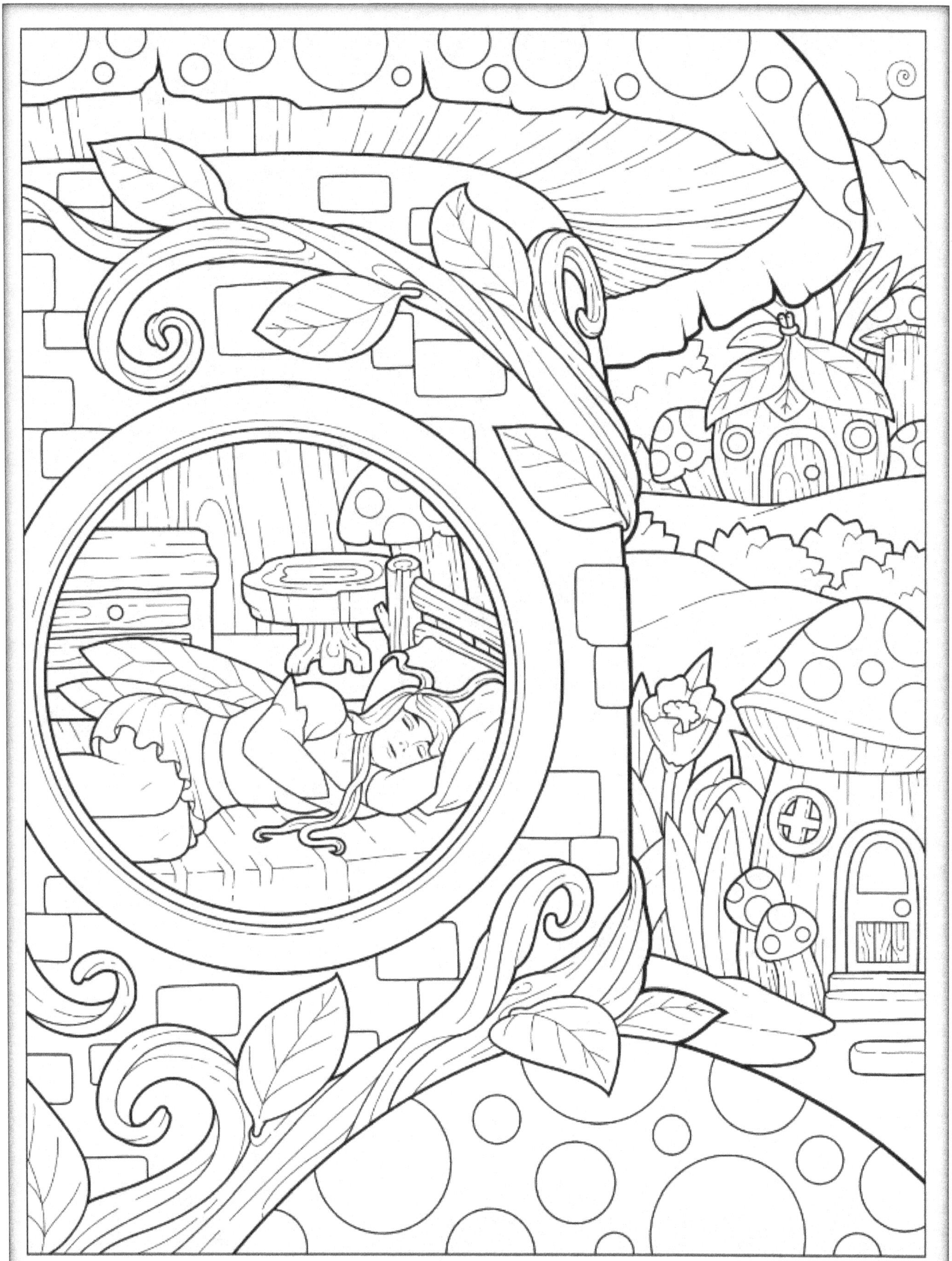

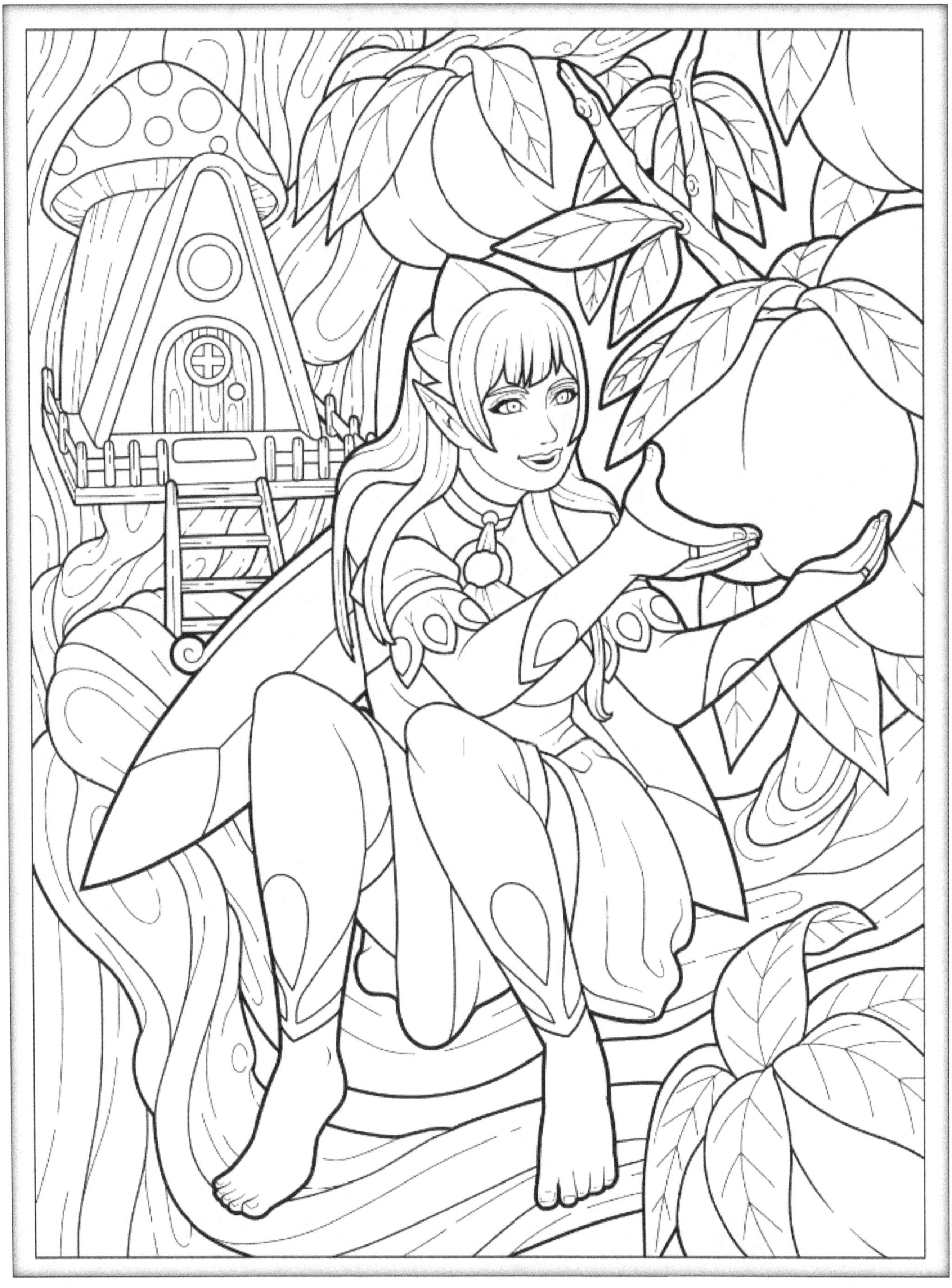

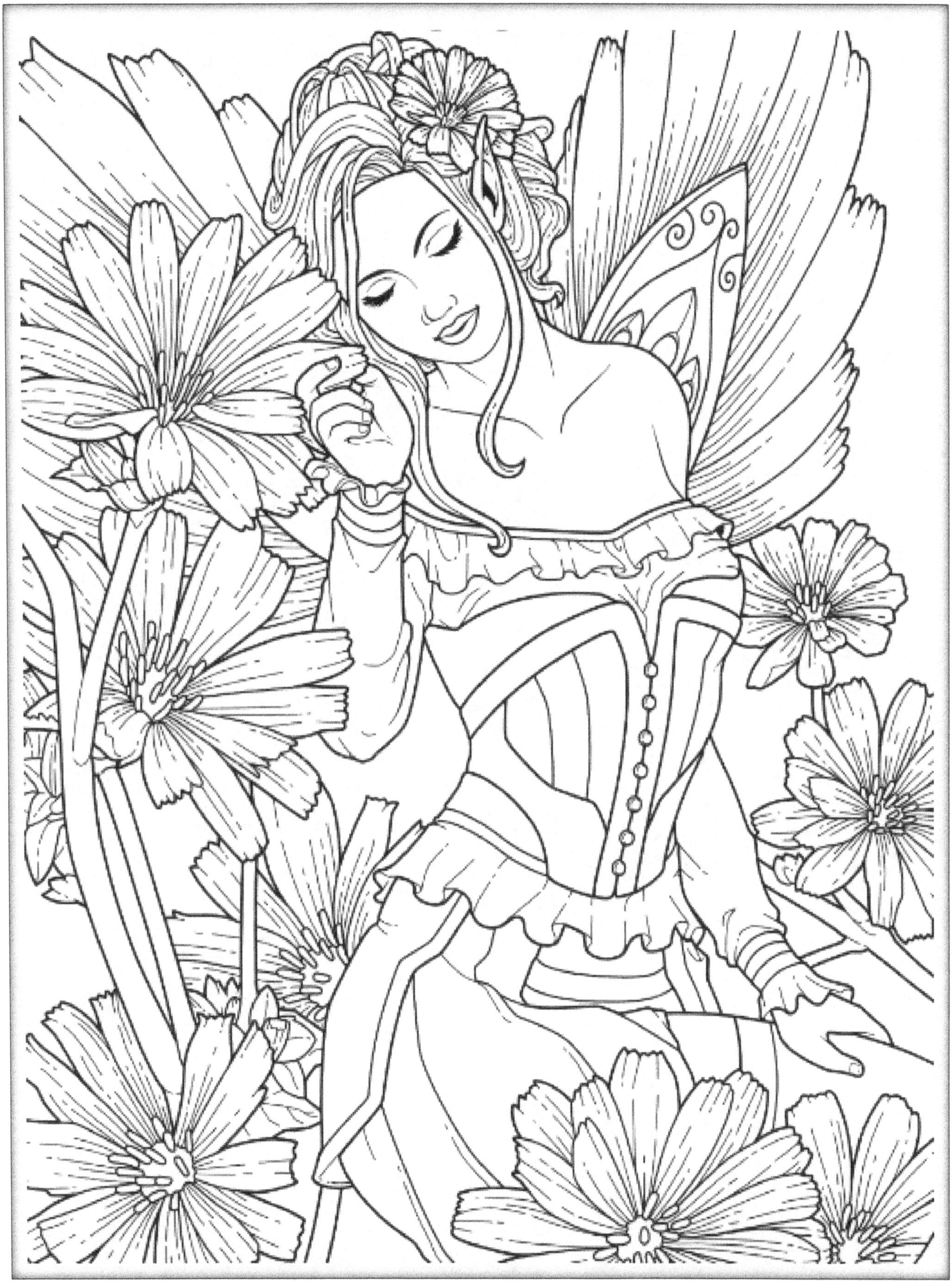

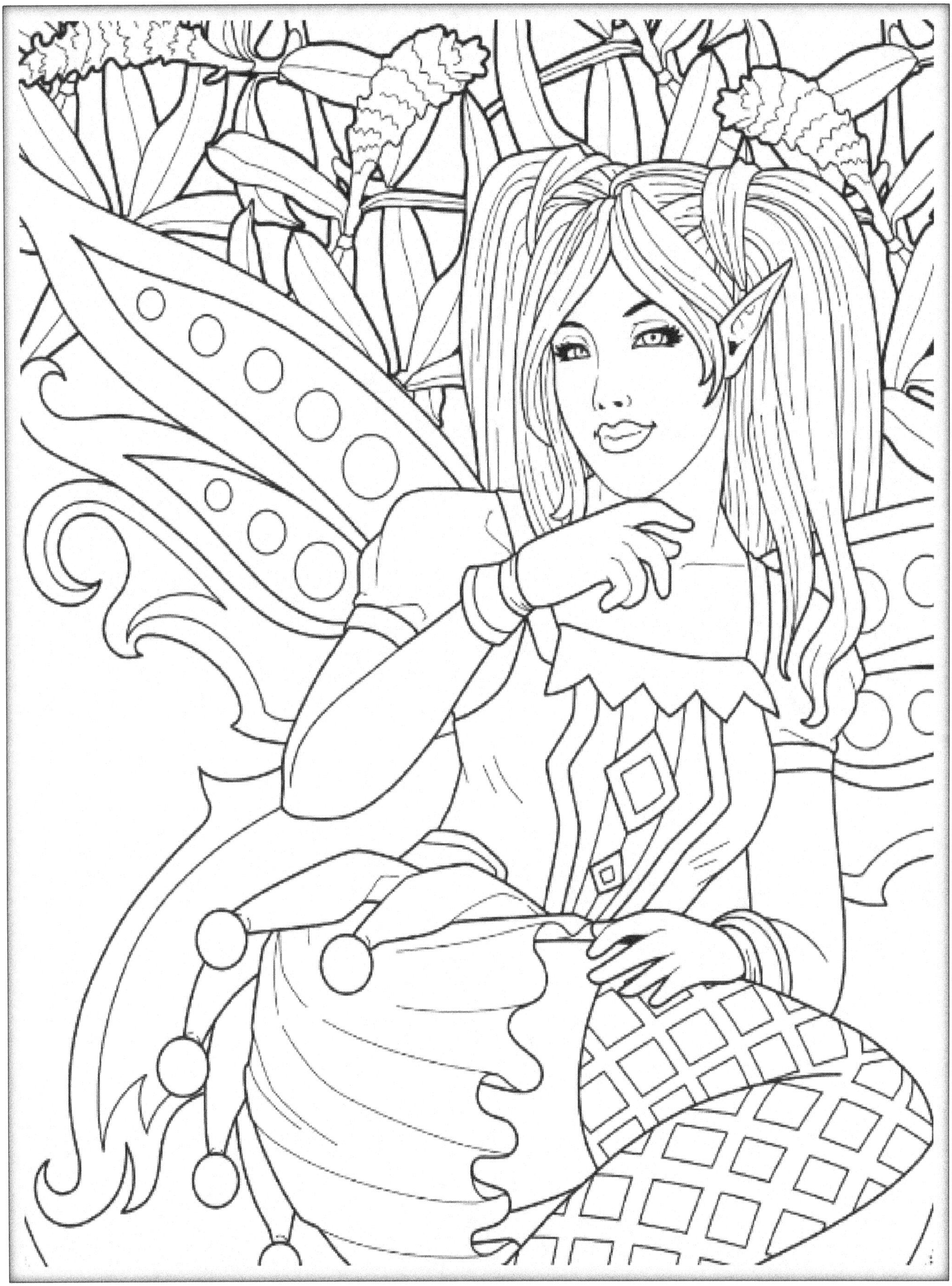

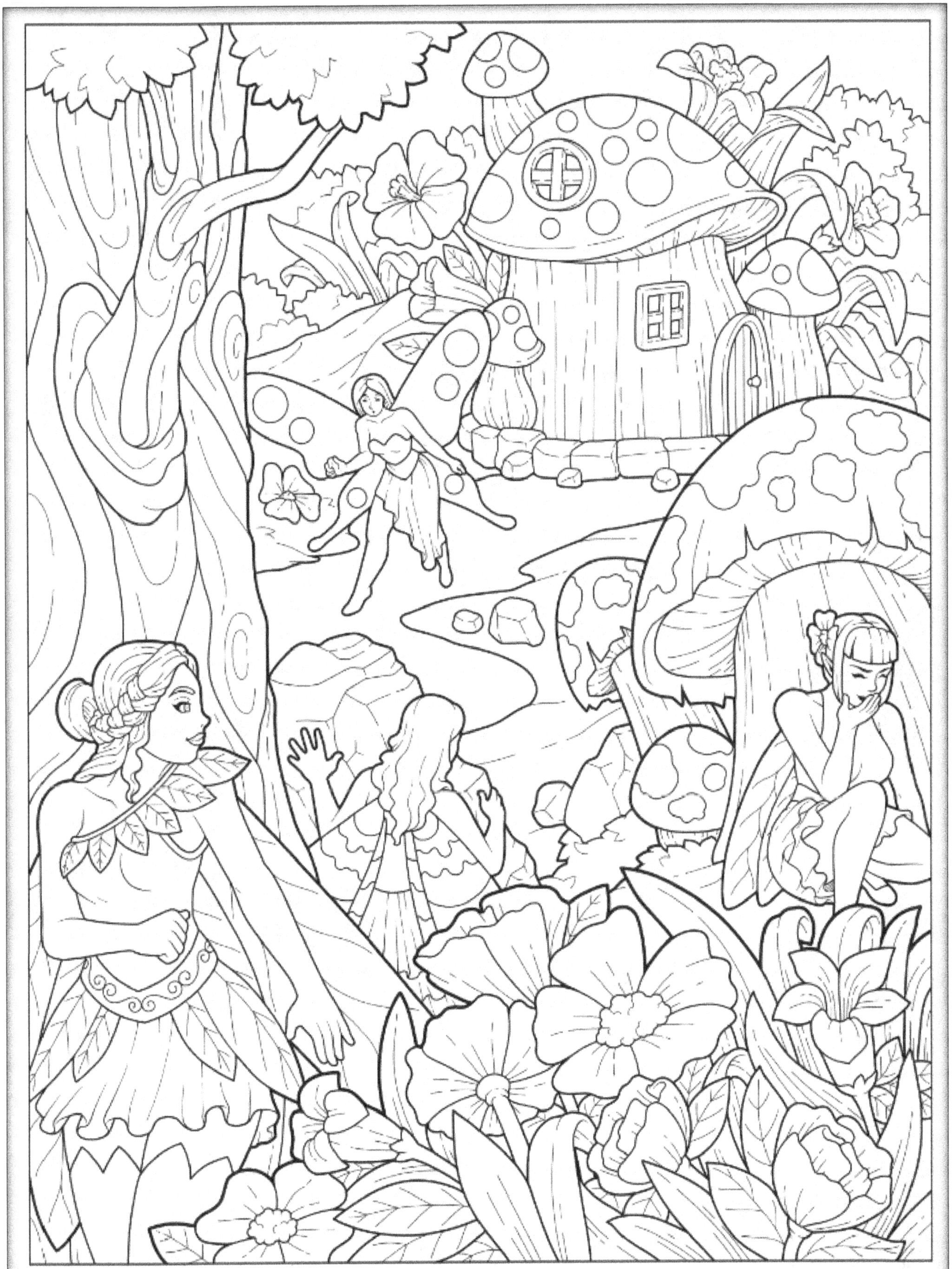

www.ingramcontent.com/pod-product-compliance
Lightning Source LLC
Chambersburg PA
CBHW081514220526
45467CB00010B/2911
* 9 7 9 8 7 0 5 8 5 5 7 0 4 *